DEDICATION

Dedicated to my daughter Cara b[

ACKNOWLEDGEMENTS

Thanks to Mike Penney for many of the photos.

ABOUT THE AUTHOR

Gordon Emery is an active footpath walker and worker. As well as helping to produce 'Walks Around Wrexham Maelor' for Clwyd County Council, and publishing his own 'Walks in Clwyd' series and 'Guide to the Maelor Way', he has been active in erecting or repairing over 900 stiles and bridges in the Wrexham area (the first 190, including those on the Maelor Way, on a voluntary basis).

His wife and two sons are also keen walkers, although his youngest son (6 years old at the time of writing) who tested the walks is happy to stop and play in a stream all day, and his eldest son (18) prefers long treks over the Lake District fells.

Fishmine (Route 14)

Family Walks
on the
North Wales Coast

Gordon Emery

HIGH INTEREST · LOW MILEAGE

Scarthin Books of Cromford
Derbyshire
1996

Family Walks Series

THE COUNTRY CODE

Guard against all risk of fire
Fasten all gates
Keep dogs under proper control
Keep to paths across farmland
Avoid damaging fences, hedges and walls
Leave no litter
Safeguard water supplies
Protect wildlife, plants and trees
Go carefully on country roads
Respect the life of the countryside

Published by Scarthin Books, Cromford, Derbyshire, 1996

Phototypesetting by Paragon Typesetters, Newton-le-Willows

Printed by Redwood Books

Maps by Ivan Sendall

Photographs by the author and by Mike Penney (Storm Photography)

Cover photograph: Mike Penney

ISBN 0 907758 89 4

Contents

Map of the North Wales Coast

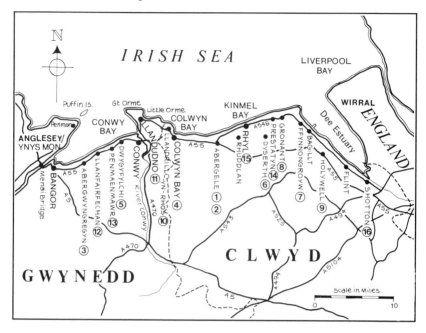

ACCESS TO THE AREA

By rail – The North Wales Coast is served by the Chester-Holyhead line. Passengers to Llandudno may have to change at Llandudno Junction. Passengers from Liverpool, Wirral or Wrexham change trains at Shotton.

By bus – Coastal buses go through all the towns shown except Dyserth (change at Prestatyn).

By road – All the towns can be reached by the A55 trunk road, branching on to the A548 for Shotton, Rhyl, Prestatyn and Ffynnongroyw; the A5151 to Dyserth and Holywell; and the B1115 to Llandrillo-yn-Rhos and Llandudno.

Introduction

This is the second book in the 'Family Walks' series that I have had the pleasure of writing. The routes in 'Family Walks in the North Wales Borderlands', which explore the valleys and hills around Wrexham and Llangollen, are very different from these coastal routes, which mostly tend to go up into the hills above the conurbations of the tourist resorts. Only a few of the walks are on reasonably flat land and these have been included for their wildlife and historical interest.

However, most of the ascents are straightforward, and easy alternatives are given to the few 'scrambles' on the main routes.

If you go on all these walks you will find that you can trace the outline of some of the others from your 'aerial' viewpoints.

As in my last guide, I have tried to include routes which will keep a child running ahead to see what is around the next corner. Taking my six-year-old on the walks was an ideal test of this.

Public transport and timing

All these walks can be reached by public transport — so why not leave your car, your cares, and your pollution at home? Children love travelling by train and bus, even if they are used to going by car. It may not be as quick, but you can make a day's outing by having a meal or picnic as well.

Take your time on the walks, especially with young children. For children under eight allow at least an hour for every mile. Walking in groups usually keeps the pace to about one-and-a-half miles an hour, but allow for a ten minute rest each hour and a half-hour break if you take a picnic.

Remember to check return transport times before you set off, and leave time to go to the beach!

Food and drink

Many of the routes have cafes or shops at the beginning (or end), but you will need to take food with you if you are likely to get hungry on the way. Hot food can be carried in a wide-necked Thermos flask or its plastic equivalent for safety.

What to wear

As long as your child's shoes are comfortable and have good grips on the soles almost any footwear is suitable. (I walked most of the routes in sandals). Do not go out and buy a pair of heavy walking boots which will need breaking in anyway and may put your child off walking for life. On the other hand some children love wearing special walking equipment and will climb with more enthusiasm, especially with some of the lightweight boots on the market today. If a pair of trainers is likely to get soaked after wet weather, or seaside wave dodging, take a spare pair and some dry socks to change into for the journey home.

It pays to be prepared. Always carry light rainwear if there is a sign of a cloud, and in winter ensure that you have extra clothing — it can be cold on the hills.

Pack a snack and lumber a jumper.

Wet weather days

It is fun to walk in the rain, but miserable if you get too wet. Choose a short route with shelter nearby. Lists of visitor centres, castles, museums, swimming pools and other useful telephone numbers are given at the back of the book.

Choosing a walk

If you are not sure of the area or how far your children will go, choose a walk from the top of the list in the appendices at the back of the book. Some of the routes include short cuts, and if you are less than half-way, never be afraid to turn back, especially in fog or bad weather.

Rights of way

As soon as you leave the public right of way you fail to be insured by the Highway Authority and are probably trespassing. (Trespass is not normally an offence unless you do damage, but owners can ask you to leave and use reasonable force if you don't.) If fields are ploughed or crops growing you should walk in single file in the right direction. If, on public rights of way, you meet an obstruction you can, by law, take the nearest route around or remove enough of it to get past.

Some of the routes which I wanted to include in this guide were too difficult due to illegal obstruction. A countryside survey showed that 80% of circular walks in Wales could not be completed because of this type of problem − perhaps one of the reasons why people buy walk guides. At the time of writing, all these 16 walks were free of major obstructions and crops (except for two fields where alternatives are given). Minor problems and missing signs have been notified to the Highway Authorities.

If you walk on any public footpaths in the area and find difficulties, please write to the County Councils and send a copy of your letter to the appropriate secretary of the Ramblers' Association (see appendices). The Council do not check the paths themselves and only look into problems when they are reported by members of the public.

Maps

No extra maps are needed for these walks, but it is worth buying them for any district you walk in regularly. The Ordnance Survey 1:25,000 Pathfinder shows paths and field boundaries. You would need nine of them to cover these routes. For the full list see the appendices.

MAP KEY

═══	Road	→-→-		Route (footpath not always evident)
═════	Track	·······		Alternative Route
- - - -	Path	■		House on the route
□	Buildings			
□ PH	Public House			Woodland
	Church	START		Start
~~	Stream or River			Viewpoint
≈≈≈	River	①		Numbers denote route directions
⊜	Pond	─┼►Z		Approximate North
⊨	Bridge			
++++	Railway			NONE OF THE MAPS ARE TO SCALE
—+—	Dismantled Railway or Tramway			Some parts of the route maps have been expanded to show directions in detail

The Watchtower

The Watchtower

Outline

Abergele — River Gele — Bronyberllan — The Watchtower —
Plas Uchaf — River Gele — Abergele

Summary

A footpath leads from the centre of the village along the riverside. The route then gradually ascends to a viewpoint at the watchtower. A choice of two wooded return routes is available. A field on the longer route may be boggy.

Attractions

The hills and valleys around Abergele are some of the most accessible on the coast and, even though the town has expanded, the path alongside the river has been kept and not incorporated into estate roads (planners take note). The large majority of the garden owners alongside the path have taken pride in having the end of their gardens open to public inspection and have planted them accordingly.

The watchtower is one of several around the coast of Britain. A system of beacons was originally put in place by Edward II, in part to warn him against the return of his unfaithful queen and her lover, Mortimer.

By 1403 Parliament had ordained that a sea watch be kept throughout the realm, and a tax named 'beconium' was levied to erect and watch beacons. The watchtower here, probably built in the 17th century, had three floors and would have flags as well as a beacon holding a bucket in which a lump of pitch was fired.

In 1803 Wheeler's Manchester Chronicle announced that 'fire beacons and flags had been tested [elsewhere] and found to answer completely', presumably in response to the threat of Napoleon. One notable recorded use for the beacons was in Elizabethan times when they were lit around the coastline at the approach of the Spanish Armada, thus giving Sir Francis Drake time to finish his game of bowls before he set out to sea.

Refreshments

The Food Bar Caffe near Pen-y-bont has a children's menu and serves vegetarian meals. There is also a take-away. Shops, and other cafes, can be found in Abergele or near the beach in Pensarn.

Route 1

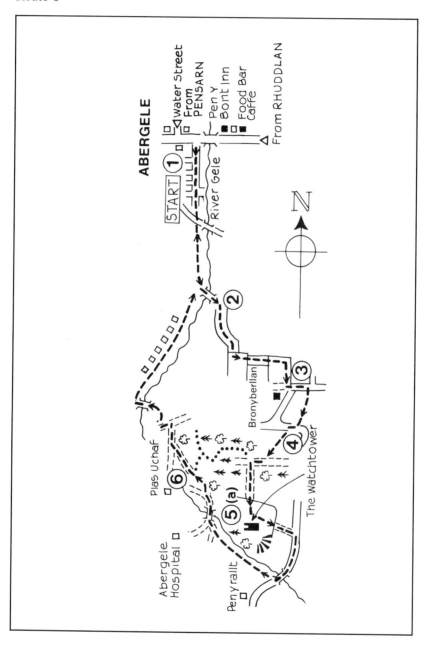

The Watchtower   3 or 4 miles

Start

Abergele, Pen-y-Bont Inn, near the junction of High Street and Water Street, GR SH947745. By train to Abergele and Pensarn, then follow the main road (Dundonald Avenue) to Abergele. Coastal buses go through the town. Car parks are signposted.

Alternatives

For the shorter route follow direction 5; for the longer route follow 5a.

Route

1. *From the inn, cross the bridge over the River Gele, then turn left and follow the lane alongside the river. Continue along the tarmac path ahead, through the park and past houses. Beyond a driveway fork left beside the stream, cross the bridge and go up the steps.*

2. *After a right turn and the short enclosed path, enter the open field and turn left along the hedge to reach a kissing gate and another enclosed path. (If this is very overgrown use the gate alongside). At the end of the path follow the dip around the field to the top corner.*

3. *Turn left at the road and after 200 metres turn right up a path opposite a road junction. Follow the dip of a hollow way to a stile.*

4. *On the lane go downhill for 30 metres, then fork left up the woodland path. At the top turn right on to a forestry track. Above the crest of the hill turn left on to another wide track which leads to the watchtower.*

5. *For the shorter return route return along the track, turn left at the T-junction and immediately right. Turn left at the next junction and right at the T-junction. Now follow direction 6.*

5a. *For the longer route find the track on the eastern edge of the field (the doorway of the watchtower faces Abergele to the north). Go through the kissing gate and follow the track to the lane. Turn right and follow the lane down to a bridge and up for 100 metres to a stile on your right. Keep by the woodland boundary on your right until you reach the bottom corner of the long field. Continue downhill on the track, turn right and right again on to the public path. Continue ahead at the next bend. Now follow direction 6.*

6. *Follow the stone track to the second corner where you should go ahead, passing disused lime kilns, to the T-junction. Turn left and, in 400 metres, cross the river. Turn right to the town.*

'Roman' steps

Gopa Wood

Outline
Abergele Library — Gopa Wood — Tyddyn Morgan — Siamber Wen — Abergele

Summary
The route follows a narrow passageway from the centre of the village. An easy or steep ascent can be taken into the woods and up to a viewpoint. After following woodland paths the descent is on a quiet lane and alongside a stream into the village.

Attractions
Gopa Wood is owned by the Woodland Trust, and in recent years volunteers have enjoyed themselves clearing paths and building steps to provide access. Much of the wood was cleared before it was sold, so that new growth has shot up providing wildlife cover.

From the viewpoint you look down on the 19th century Gwrych Castle, a 'folly' built by the local estate owner Lloyd Bamford-Hesketh and based on his own drawings. In 1919, the castle was bequeathed to George V, together with £50,000 for its upkeep, but he refused the bequest. Jewish refugees were housed there in the Second World War and since then it has been allowed to fall into ruin. Some local people claim that public paths run past the building.

A bridge spans 'Devil's Gorge', a former lead or calcite open-cast mine. Beside it are the 'Roman Steps', but these are likely to be of 18th or 19th century origin.

The ramparts of Castell Cawr (giant's castle) can be found in the woodland, but were probably more impressive before the woodland was planted. The name Gopa gives a clue to the hill's shape before afforestation, as it comes from the Saxon meaning a button or protrusion. The castle is the ruin of an Iron Age 'Celtic' hillfort, so you are unlikely to meet any giants.

Refreshments
There are a few eating places in the village. The cafe or take-away next to the Peny-y-Bont Inn has a children's menu and also serves vegetarian meals.

Route 2

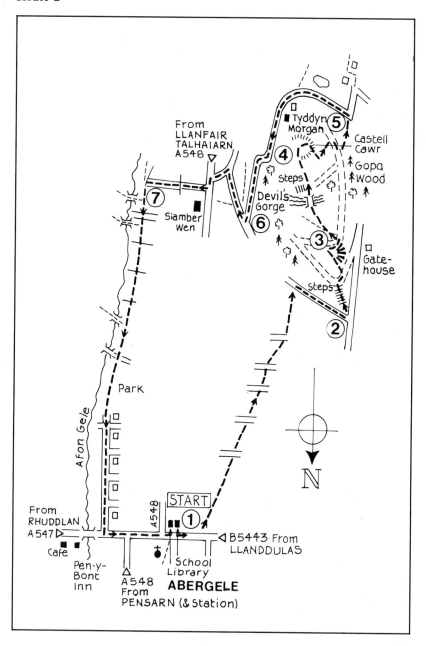

16

Route 2

Gopa Wood   3 miles

Start

Abergele Library, GR SH944776. Some coastal trains stop at Abergele and Pensarn Station. Take a bus into the village or follow the main road (Dundonald Avenue). Coastal buses serve the village and there is a car park in the centre. From the centre the library is along the main road heading towards Colwyn Bay.

Alternatives

Substitutes to two short scrambles are given in brackets.

Route

1. *Go past the school and take the footpath on your left in 20 metres. Continue along several sections of this path to reach a lane below the hillside. Turn right.*

2. *By the road junction turn left up a stepped path. At the track turn right and immediately left. (The easier alternative is to turn left at the track, follow it uphill, then turn right).*

3. *At the corner viewpoint climb up the rocky path on your left. (To avoid this short scramble continue along the track, then turn sharp left on to a green track and right at the next path. Go on to direction 4). Fork right at the junction and eventually cross the bridge over 'Devil's Gorge'. Do not turn down the path on your left unless you wish to see the 'Roman Steps', but fork left at the next junction.*

4. *Do not fork left downhill at the clearing, but continue to follow the path which bears right through the overgrown ramparts of the hillfort. Turn left at the T-junction.*

5. *Turn right at the track and left down steps in 100 metres. Turn left at the next track.*

6. *At the foot of the hill, beyond Tyddyn Morgan, turn right at the lane, then left at the road junction. Cross the main road and take the path diagonally opposite.*

7. *Before the river turn left and follow the path, then the road ahead to the town centre. Turn left to the library.*

Rhaeadr Fawr

Aber Falls

Outline
Abergwyngregyn — Bont Newydd — Nant — waterfalls —
Cae'r Mynydd — Abergwyngregyn

Summary
The public footpath up to the falls is a wide track. From there the path is more rugged and ascends on to the hillside for a more panoramic return journey.

Attractions
See if you can spot the old mill leat beside the lane in Aber(gwyngregyn). It took water from the river to the village mill.

The track to the falls is the easiest part of this breathtakingly beautiful walk on the edge of Snowdonia National Park. The Aber valley is a national nature reserve and access to the falls has been made easy, in part to stop further intrusion into the valley.

You could be forgiven for wondering what the nature trail posts 1, 2 and 3 refer to. Initial impressions might be: 1. A solid block of conifers topped by electricity pylons. 2. Inappropriate fencing instead of stone walls. 3. Yet more conifers, fences and falling-down walls with a concrete drain nearby, added to round it off. Further poor planning reveals itself in the shape of ugly wire cages used to prevent erosion near the waterfall.

However, you can stop at The Nant visitor centre to see their exhibition, pick up a leaflet on 'Coedydd Aber' which includes the nature trail, and hope that further work in the valley might take the scenery into consideration.

The rocky stream below Rhaeadr Fawr (great waterfall) makes a wonderful playground for children under supervision, so take a towel if your family enjoy paddling. Beyond the waterfall this route leaves the well-trodden tourist route and heads up, albeit under the pylons, to a magnificent viewpoint 250 metres above sea level.

From here the impressive views encompass Bera Mawr (with the slightly taller Bera Bach behind) to the west of the waterfall, Llwyntmor to the east. On the rear ridge opposite are Drum (Carnedd Pendorth-goch) and Carnedd y Ddelw, with the screes of Foel Ganol in the forefront. Along the rear ridge, towards the sea, is Carreg Fawr with Penmaenmawr near the coast and Great Orme in the distance. Leading up from the valley is a winding lane, a former drovers' road from Anglesey to England, based on the Roman road that preceded it. This itself was probably on a Celtic way used by the Druids, before the Romans invaded Anglesey and smashed their holy groves.

Refreshments
The Aber Falls Hotel is open most of the day for a variety of food and drink.

Route 3

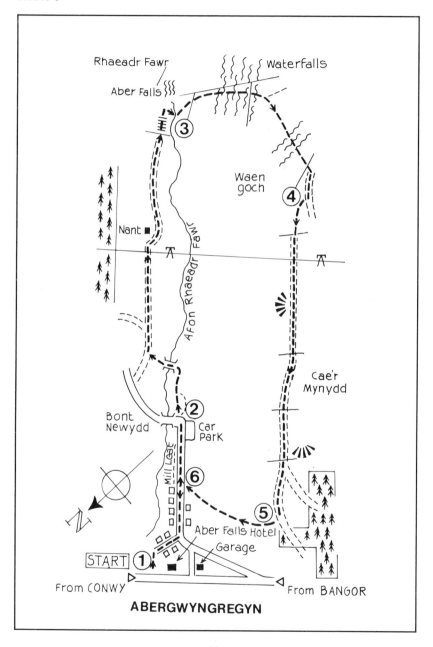

Route 3

Aber Falls   4 or 5 miles

Start

Abergwyngregyn, Aber Falls Hotel. Nearest station Bangor. Regular buses from Bangor to Llandudno. Car parking for patrons. GR SH656727.

Alternative Start

Car park at Bont Newydd, Aber. GR SJ662720 (start from direction 2).

Alternatives

If you want a gentle walk, or feel unable to cross the stream below the waterfall, return by the same path, but then you miss the best views.

Route

1. *Take the signposted path beside the hotel. Continue along the road, turn left at the T-junction and head up the lane to Bont Newydd.*

2. *From the car park before the bridge, follow the streamside path. In 200 metres cross the footbridge and follow the track, forking right at the next junction.*

3. *In a mile cross the stream below the falls. Use the (waymarked) stile and follow the path below the wall. Cross the next three streams, a ladder stile and another stream, then fork right. Beyond two more streams the path heads up through a wet gap in the drystone wall, then levels out for only a hundred metres.*

4. *Fork right on to the lower path (waymarked) and, beyond another ladder stile, the green way is clear for over a mile.*

5. *As you come in sight of the road, just after a gateway, take the right fork downhill. Before the trees turn sharp right along the narrow (waymarked) path.*

6. *At the lane turn left to the village (or right to Bont Newydd car park).*

Dinosaur World

Pwllycrochan Woods and Nant-y-Glyn

Outline
Colwyn Bay Station — Pwllychrochan Woods — Foxhill — Nant-y-Glyn —
Cilgwyn Mawr — Colwyn Bay

Summary
A steady ascent takes you to woodland above the town and into Nant-y-Glyn. Ascend
the hill for views of the bay. Parts of the route may be muddy.

Attractions
Not only is Colwyn Bay the home of the Welsh Mountain Zoo, but also Dinosaur
World, predecessor to Jurassic Park. A variety of imaginatively coloured monsters
from the Cretaceous, Jurassic and Triassic ages wander around Erias Park, but none
have escaped yet! Please remember to close the gate when leaving.

The walk ascends past Victorian buildings to Pwllcrochan Woods, now owned
by the Town Council and open to the public. The Pwllycrochan Estate once belonged
to the Erskine family who packed their bags and moved to their larger Scottish estate,
having, by the terms of a will, to reside there for part of the year anyway. The four
day sale in 1865 put much of the 1,200 hectares in the hands of John Pender, a
merchant who was later knighted for financially backing the laying of the first
transatlantic cable. His agent opened Pwllycrochan as a hotel. A Manchester syndicate
bought most of the estate ten years later, and this, combined with the new railway
station, led to a rapid rise in the town's development. By 1891 the population had
reached nearly five thousand, and by 1913 Colwyn Bay was the largest town on the
North Wales coast.

The main part of the walk is above Nant-y-Glyn (both nant and glyn translate as
valley). The walk ascends to Cilgwyn Mawr, an old farmstead from where there is
a possibility of going further uphill for better views of the bay.

Refreshments
Shops, cafes and restaurants can be found in the town. There are also cafes at the zoo
and at Erias Park. The viewpoint shown on the map is a good place for picnics, but
remember to take all cans and bags home.

Route 4

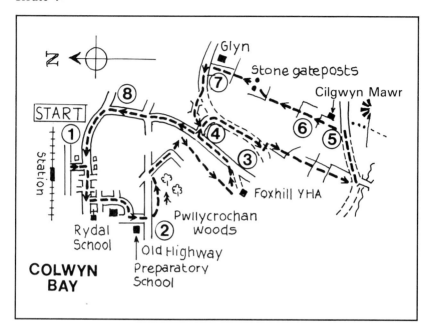

Glyn

Stone gateposts

Cilgwyn Mawr

START

Station

Foxhill YHA

Rydal
School

Pwllycrochan
woods

Old Highway

**COLWYN
BAY**

Preparatory
School

Route 4

Pwllycrochan Woods and Nant-y-Glyn   2½ or 4 miles

Start

Colwyn Bay Railway Station, GR SH850791. Coastal trains and buses. Town car parks.

Alternatives

Once you reach the woods you can explore the paths at your leisure, although the main route soon leaves the woodland and heads for Nant-y-Glyn. The short cut returns from Foxhill Youth Hostel (direction 3) and does not ascend on to the hills.

Route

1. *At the top of the pedestrian precinct turn right to Queen's Drive, just before the small park and church. Follow the drive up past the 19th century Rydal School. Around the corner, turn left at the T-junction to pass the preparatory school and, at the next T-junction, cross Old Highway into the woods.*

2. *Immediately turn left and follow the path parallel to the road. (You can explore paths in the woods and return to this path to continue). After the path rejoins Old Highway, fork right up a track. Ignore tracks and paths to right and left, but, at the corner, take the path ahead.*

3. *At the lane by Foxhill Youth Hostel turn left. When the lane heads uphill: for the short cut continue ahead (see direction 8); for the main route fork right and follow the track.*

4. *Do not take the stile on your left, but stay on the track and turn right at the junction. In 350 metres go ahead through the gate and, when the track reaches a gap in the hedgerow, go on to the open hillside. Gradually ascend to the trees ahead and take the iron kissing gate 20 metres below the corner. Cross the wet area by the well and stay under the hedge to find a metal bar stile and a woodland path beside a ruin. At the track turn left uphill.*

5. *In 400 metres turn left over the stile before the barns (unless you wish to ascend the path on your right just beyond the farm to gain extra height − there is a good view from the top of the first field).*

6. *Descend beside the barn and over another stile, then veer slightly right to another above a gate. Follow the green track (from the stile, not the gate). Beyond the next gate, follow the upper boundary through trees, then drop down to go between two stone gateposts. Go towards the farm through iron kissing gates.*

7. *Turn left on to the lane. From the first corner drop down, cross the bridge and rejoin the outward route. At the top lane, a right turn heads for the town.*

8. *When you reach the main road, turn left to the town centre.*

Flint Castle

26

Alltwen, Penmaenbach and Mynydd y Dref

Outline
Dwygyfylchi − Coed Pendyffryn − (Alltwen & Penmaen-bach summits) − Mynydd
y Dref − Conwy − Bwlch Sychnant − Dwygyfylchi

Summary
A streamside path heads up into woodland, then steeply on to a pass between the first
two summits; short paths lead to both. The shorter route then descends back to the
village, while the longer routes head over the many peaks of Mynydd y Dref and
descend to Conwy. Unless a return is made by bus, the longest route returns through
Bwlch Sychnant, on a clear track half-way up the mountain, but more sheltered than
the outward path.

Attractions
Budding botanists should note the Irish or Fastigiate Yew trees, with their upturned
branches, in the cemetery. These trees, which can be found in cemeteries nationwide,
are all clones of the original mutated yew and can only be propagated by cuttings and
not by seed.
    Start in the morning and ascend nearly 200 metres between Alltwen and Penmaen-
bach (the summits are optional) before you decide whether to return on the short
route. Take the day to complete the longest, or at least reach Conwy.

The paths over Mynydd y Dref (Conwy Mountain) have beautiful views of the heather
moors and tops, and you can look across to the Great Orme and westwards to
Anglesey. On the summit of the mountain is the ruin of an Iron Age hillfort, Castell
Caer Seion. Views of Conwy and its impressive medieval castle can be seen on the
way down to the town.
    The quayside with its trawlers, moored sailing boats and river trips is interesting
in itself, but then there is the chance to visit Britain's 'smallest house', complete with
ticket vendor in Welsh dress, as well as the castle. The National Trust open
Aberconwy House, in the town centre, to the public, and there is also a Visitor Centre,
whilst on the outside of the walled town is the Butterfly Jungle (see appendices for
opening times and further information).
    When you have had enough of the town head back along the old road to Bwlch
Sychnant, or if trekking round the town has worn the family out, take the bus.

Refreshments
Take a snack with you to eat on the summit, but when you reach Conwy there are
heaps of chip shops. More varied fare can be had at The River Grill Restaurant
(licensed) in Berry Street who cater for vegetarians and vegans, have a children's
menu or can even supply you with sandwiches for the walk back.

Route 5

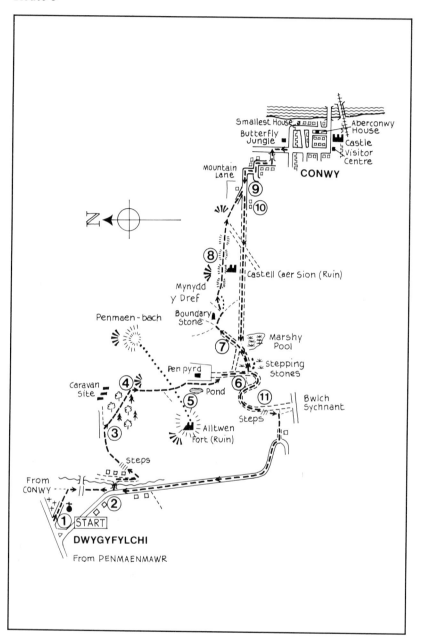

Smallest House · Aberconwy House · Butterfly Jungle · Castle · Visitor Centre · **CONWY**

Mountain Lane

⑨ ⑩

⑧ Castell Caer Sion (Ruin)

Mynydd y Dref

Penmaen-bach Boundary Stone

Marshy Pool

⑦ Stepping Stones

Pen pyrd

Caravan Site ④ ⑥

⑤ Pond ⑪ Bwlch Sychnant

③ Steps

Alltwen Fort (Ruin)

Steps

From CONWY

② Steps

① START

DWYGYFYLCHI

From PENMAENMAWR

28

Route 5

Alltwen, Penmaenbach and Mynydd y Dref   2, 4 or 7 miles

Start

Dwygyfylchi Church, GR SH736773. Trains to Llandudno Junction, then take the bus from the flyover roundabout. Coastal buses stop by the church. Parking in lanes nearby.

Alternatives

These are clearly marked in the text, so there is no need to decide how far to walk before you set out. The walk is extended by a mile if you climb the first two summits (see direction 4). The longer walks go over a third summit to Conwy, only four miles if you return by bus.

Route

1. *Follow the footpath between the church and the cemetery. Turn right at the T-junction and soon cross a driveway.*

2. *Turn left at the road and immediately cross the footbridge on your left. Turn right and, at the end of the track, follow the footpath up behind the houses.*

3. *In the woodland of Scots pines, as the path descends beside the fence, take the second right fork, keeping you 100 metres above the caravans. Ignore the next track down to the left.*

4. *Above the wood fork right. As the steep path levels out ignore a right turn, but in a few metres, at the cross paths, you can turn right to the summit of Alltwen, or left to the summit of Penmaen-bach, returning to the cross paths to continue the route ahead.*

5. *Pass the pond on your right and the farm on your left, then go ahead along the farm track for 150 metres.*

6. *For the short route stay on the track and follow direction 11. For the longer routes to Conwy turn left up the (signposted) path, using the stepping stones just past it.*

7. *Cross the wide track by the marshy pool, but turn right at the next cross paths to pass a small boundary stone. Now keep ahead to ascend the main path on the seaward side of the mountain until you reach the summit. (In fog this is difficult to recognise as there are several small peaks. Just make sure you do not turn to your left.)*

8. *Descend over the smaller peaks until, in about a mile, you reach the lane. Turn left to Conwy, or right if you wish to return and miss out the town (follow direction 10).*

9. *Turn left at the T-junction on the estate road and right at the main road to visit Conwy, returning to this point to continue the route.*

10.*Follow the lower stony track beside the wall and, in half a mile, stay on the higher track when the bridleway falls away to your left. In about a mile you reach the marshy pool on your outward route. Turn left and, across the stepping stones, turn left on to the farm track.*

11.*Before the road take the valley path down to your right. At the lane continue down to the village and retrace your steps along the streamside path to the church.*

The Ship, Bagillt Quay

Graig Fawr

Outline
Dyserth Waterfall − old leat − Graig Fawr − Prestatyn Walkway −
Dyserth Waterfall

Summary
The route ascends steps near the waterfall, then follows a level path and, after a small valley and another level path, a short steep ascent takes you to the viewpoint on the summit. The return route uses a disused railway line, now the Prestatyn Walkway.

Attractions
The Dyserth Waterfall is a popular attraction and, although there is a small admission charge towards the upkeep of the grounds, it is well worth watching the seven tonnes of water per minute that cascade down the 20 metre drop in the 'Dyserth Stream' (actually the Afon Ffyddion) which flows from Ffynnon Asa (St Asaph's well).

After the steps and the stream crossing, the path joins an old leat, now dry, which was built in 1754 and carried water to power waterwheels and wash lead ores at the Meliden mines. Once across the valley, the path follows the same leat. Mines in the area have been worked since at least Roman times, although the earliest recorded mining took place here in the 14th century. Across the fields is the tall ruin of the Clive Engine House where a gigantic steam engine, with a 2 metre diameter cylinder, pumped water from the mines from 1860 until 1884, when cheap imports of lead made the business uneconomical.

Graig Fawr (big crag) consists of carboniferous limestone which, after earth movement in the Silurian Age, gained deposits of minerals from their solutions in sea water. The rough lane on the hill bears the scars from open-cast mines and also from its use as a tank recovery training ground in the Second World War. Nevertheless, time has healed old wounds, and the grass-covered slopes have become a haven for limestone-loving plants. The whole area belongs to the National Trust.

The Prestatyn Walkway lies on the former course of the Dyserth Railway owned by L & NWR. Nine trains a day once ran along this single-track line and safety was assured with the possession of a wooden staff by the driver of the train with right of way. After mineral traffic ceased the line was closed in 1930.

Refreshments
The Waterfalls Cafe serves snacks, drinks, chips and meals all day. Opposite is the Red Lion/Llew Coch which has a children's menu. The hill is ideal for a picnic on a sunny day, but, as always, please take litter back with you.

31

Route 6

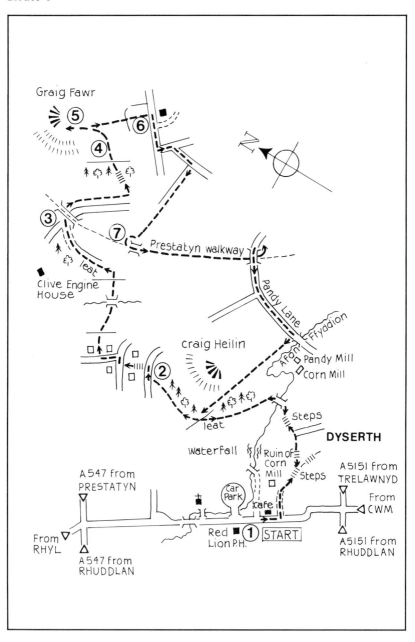

Graig Fawr

⑤ ⑥

④

③ ⑦ Prestatyn walkway

leat

Clive Engine House

Pandy Lane

Ffyddion

Craig Heilin

② Afon Pandy Mill
Corn Mill

leat

Steps

DYSERTH

Waterfall

Ruin of Corn Mill

Steps

A547 from PRESTATYN

A5151 from TRELAWNYD

From CWM

Car Park

Cafe

From RHYL

A547 from RHUDDLAN

Red Lion P.H. ① START

A5151 from RHUDDLAN

Route 6

Graig Fawr   2 miles

Start

Dyserth Waterfalls (signposted), GR SJ056794. Trains and buses on the coast line run to Prestatyn, from where you can catch the frequent bus (not as frequent in the evenings) to Dyserth. Parking is available next to the waterfall.

Route

1. *From the waterfall entrance turn up the road and into the roadway beside the shop. Climb the steps and ignore forks to the right. At the lane turn left, descend and cross the stream. Above it your path joins the old leat.*

2. *When you reach the lane turn right, then left down a short path on to an estate road. Turn right, then left to find the path leaving the estate. Turn half-right across the field, using the concrete bridge and a stile. Turn left and ascend slightly to follow the wooded path below the wall, on the leat again.*

3. *Cross the lane and turn right through the brick archway under the Prestatyn Walkway. Go up stone steps and head along the path beside the lane. In 100 metres turn left up the stepped path on to Graig Fawr.*

4. *Continue beyond the trees and bear half-left up a grass slope to reach the summit.*

5. *From the summit head south-east towards a large cream and white house with three chimney stacks in the distance. (If visibility is poor, retrace your steps down from the summit, but keep straight on when the path forks).*

6. *A kissing gate takes you on to the road. Turn right, then take the first lane on the left and go immediately right. Take the first footpath on your right after 100 metres and descend to the Prestatyn Walkway. (From here you can retrace your steps across the valley or continue).*

7. *Once on the Walkway turn left. By the overhead bridge ascend steps to Pandy Lane. Turn left. Ignore the lane on your right, but take the next path on your right just beyond it. At the end of the path cross the meadow ahead, then descend to the path on the leat. Turn left and retrace your steps to Dyserth.*

Garth Mill, Ffynnongroew

Garth Wood

Outline
Ffynnongroyw − Garth Mill − Wern − McWalters' Dingle −
Garth Mill − Ffynnongroyw

Summary
A quiet woodland path rises to nearly 100 metres above sea level. From here a level track follows the brow of the hill, and then the route descends through a field and through woodland.

Attractions
This must be one of the most pleasant woodland walks along the coast. The woodland contains a diversity of plants and trees and is now owned by the Woodland Trust. Look out for hemp agrimony, a tall pink-flowered plant, by the riverside, as well as Himalayan balsam, now a common sight near water. Further up the path the twin yellow-flowered cow-wheat has seeds that, if they get mixed with flour, turn the mixture black.

The fine stems of wood-mellick, a grass, can be found on the shady slopes, while on the return journey you have to pass through archways of the tall pendulous sedge.

Look also for varied trees, especially sweet chestnut which casts its small but edible chestnuts on to the woodland floor in autumn.

Refreshments
Garth Mill is a public house, although there is no hanging sign, and liquid refreshment is available during opening hours. The field above the wood is ideal for picnics, especially on a warm summer day. Cool clear water gushes from a spring on the return woodland path through McWalters' Dingle.

Route 7

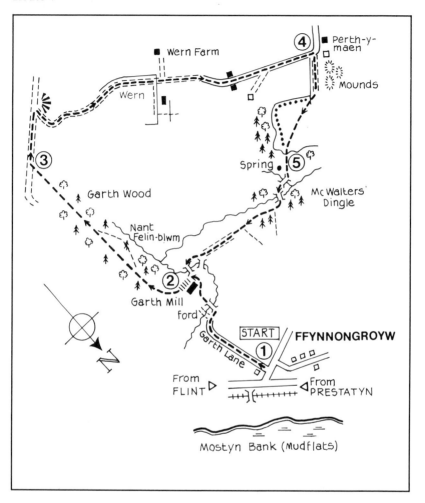

Wern Farm

Perth-y-maen

Mounds

Wern

Garth Wood

Spring ⑤

Mc Walters' Dingle

③

Nant Felin-blwm

N

② Garth Mill ford

Garth Lane

START ①

FFYNNONGROYW

From FLINT ▷

◁ From PRESTATYN

Mostyn Bank (Mudflats)

Garth Wood

2½ miles

Start

Ffynnongroyw, at the eastern end of the village opposite the pedestrian railway bridge, GR SJ141820. The nearest train station is Prestatyn. Coastal buses pass through the village. Park cars on the main street.

Route

1. *From the junction of the A548 and the Ffynnongroyw Road (both signed) take Garth Lane.*

2. *Beyond Garth Mill turn immediately left and left again up steps behind the building. Keep to the main path above the river for over half a mile.*

3. *At the track beyond the woodland turn right. Go through the gate, turn right and follow the track. Beyond the house stay on the straight track. Go through more gates at Trelogan-uchaf and proceed along the tarmac lane.*

4. *At the sharp left bend, by a house, turn right along the track beside mounds. Follow the fence around to your right and go through the gateway. The legal path veers half-left across the large field, but if obstructed by a crop in summer you may have to follow the woodland edge ahead. Either way you reach the far bottom corner of the field and a stile into the wood.*

5. *Descend the path, pass the spring, and cross two streams. Ignore paths to the left and you eventually reach Garth Mill near the start of the walk.*

Worn out

37

Foelnant Telegraph Station

38

Foelnant Telegraph Station

Outline
Gronant – Coed Bell – Foelnant – radio mast – Gronant

Summary
From just outside Prestatyn a path leads from the village of Gronant on to the hills above. There is a choice of return routes, by country lane or bridleway.

Attractions
The views from these hills are unobstructed to the seaward side, so that not only has the hill been used in this century for the radio masts, but also since 1817 for telegraph. The Foelnant Telegraph Station was erected here in 1841. A system of semaphore from three masts, or lights at night, was used to carry messages about shipping from Holyhead via other stations at Llanrhyddlad, Point Lynos, Puffin Island, Great Orme and Llysfaen before coming to this point and being signalled to Bidston and on to Liverpool.

Rising through woodland beside the telegraph station, walkers pass three carved stones, the top one, marked S.E.W, is certainly an old boundary between parishes, but the tall stone in the wood may be a private boundary stone or even a gravestone.

One of the public paths from the village was obstructed at the time of writing and so a customary path into the first woodland, Coed Bell, is used instead. The legal right of way is shown on the map and this problem has been reported to the Highways Authority. Walkers finding obstructions on any of the routes in this book or any other public paths along the coast are requested to write to the council concerned (see appendices).

Refreshments
There is an inn in the village and plenty of cafes in nearby Prestatyn. A good picnic spot is by the pond at the highest point of the walk, but please leave not a trace of your visit behind.

Route 8

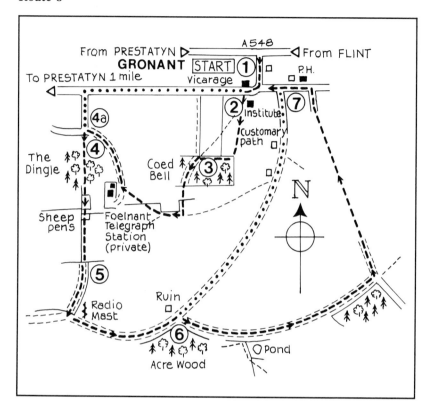

Route 8

Foelnant Telegraph Station   2, 3 or 5 miles

Start

Gronant, on the main road A548, GR SJ092834. The nearest station is Prestatyn. Coastal buses stop on the main road and there are lay-bys for cars.

Alternatives

For the shorter route follow direction 4a; for the choice of longer routes see direction 6.

Route

1. *Ascend the signposted road into the village. Beyond the prominent Institute and Bowling Green gates take steps up the footpath on your left opposite the Vicarage.*

2. *The right of way goes through the gap in the far hedge and into the wood at the next fence, but at the time of writing it was obstructed, so enter the wood by the protruding corner stile and follow the lower boundary.*

3. *In 250 metres, by a stile on your right, turn half-left up the wide green track and continue straight ahead when you leave the wood. Enter the bracken-covered hillside and turn right beyond the fence corner. From the next fence corner fork right, and right at the drive by the telegraph station (now private).*

4a. *For the shortest route, before the gateway turn down the path, turning right at the lane to Gronant.*

4. *For the longer routes turn left and ascend through the blackthorn bushes on a hollow way. Beyond the standing stone stay inside the woodland boundary, proceeding up through sheep pens and continuing to a stile on the horizon.*

5. *Stay on the track (a county road!) using stiles until you reach the radio mast. Turn left.*

6. *By the ruin fork left to Gronant or right for the longest route, which goes on to reach a track T-junction, then turns left to Gronant.*

7. *At the village road turn left.*

St. Winefride's Well

St Winefride's Well and Basingwerk Abbey

Outline
Holywell — (St Winefride's Well) — Greenfield Mill site — Abbey Wire Mill site — Visitor Centre & Farm Museum — Basingwerk Abbey — Holywell

Summary
A gentle gradient along clear tracks and paths in the Greenfield Valley. The route visits a number of ruins from several centuries.

Attractions
A number of religious, industrial and wildlife sites have been developed into the Greenfield Valley Heritage Park. This walk visits all of them, so leave time to explore.

Mosaic, in the subway leading from the town to the valley, shows the story of the seventh century St Winefride. Her suitor Caradoc, angry at being rejected, is said to have cut through Winefride's neck. Legend tells that a spring arose by her severed head which was placed next to her body by her uncle (later St Beuno), who prayed for her. She was miraculously brought back to life, while Caradoc was swallowed into the ground. Winefride became a nun, and St Winefride's Well became a focal point for pilgrims throughout the centuries.

Nearby, in the mid-twelfth century, Cistercian monks built the abbey (although the abbey was founded by the Benedictine Order). They developed the valley into a thriving community, with corn and fulling mills using the flow of water from the well as a free power source. After Henry VIII's dissolution of the monasteries in 1536, lead was stripped from the roof, the large Jesse Window was taken to Llanrhaeadr-ym-Mochnant, whilst a roof from the refectory was taken to Cilcain Church, fulfilling an earlier prophecy by a seer, Robin Ddu, who said that it would do very nicely in a little church under Moel Famau.

Industry took over the valley. Lead smelting, wire mills, a corn mill, a pin mill, a snuff mill, a paper mill and cotton mills had been introduced by the end of the 18th century, some using stone from the abbey ruins.

By the 19th century Holywell was the largest town in Flintshire. However, by the time the railway was built in 1869 local industry was in a recession. Steam power had taken over from water so that large mills were being built near deep water ports and cities. The ruins that remain only reflect the area's industrial past.

The history and archaeology of the area is told in greater detail in the Visitor Centre and in 'The Greenfield Valley', a booklet available there.

Refreshments
There is a tea shop by the bus station and several take-aways in the town. The Royal Oak Inn, passed on the walk, serves liquid refreshment, has a picnic area, and welcomes children.

Route 9

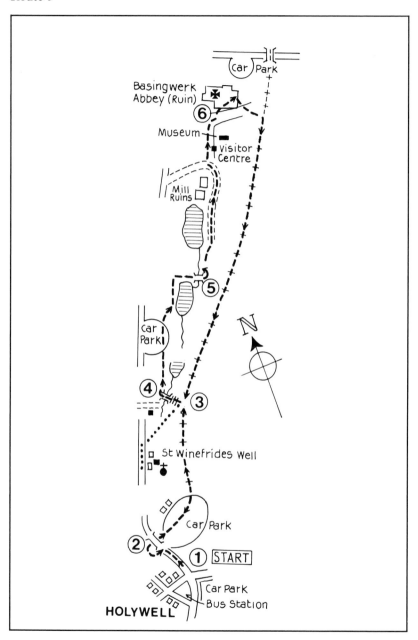

Route 9

St Winefride's Well and Basingwerk Abbey   3 miles

Start
   *Bus station, Holywell, GR 187758. Buses from Chester to Rhyl. Nearest station
   Flint, then bus to Holywell. Car park opposite.*

Alternative
   *The short walk to the holy well is shown as an addition to the main route — see
   direction 3.*

Route
1. *From the bus station follow the main road downhill towards the signposted St
   Winefride's Well.*

2. *In 50 yards use the underpass and, near the end of the car park, turn left and go
   under the bridge (the site of Holywell station). In half-a-mile turn sharp left on to
   another wide path.*

3. *Turn immediately right down the stepped path — unless you wish to visit St
   Winefride's Well by continuing to the end of the path and turning left at the road,
   returning to the stepped path to continue the main route.*

4. *From the car park before the Royal Oak, turn right and follow the stream. Pass
   the dam and the site of Greenfield Mills, go through another car park and across
   the next dam.*

5. *Across the bridge turn sharp left, down steps, to pass another reservoir and the
   Lower Cotton Mill on your left. Pass the site of the Abbey Wire Mill and, at the
   corner, turn right through the kissing gate.*

6. *Beyond the Visitor Centre and Farm Museum a kissing gate leads into Basingwerk
   Abbey. After exploring, find the corner gate behind the wooden-roofed building
   and take the steps opposite. Turn right along the former railway track, and ascend
   gradually to the town.*

The River Clwyd at Rhyl

Bryn Euryn

Outline
Llandrillo-yn-Rhos Church — The Ship — Llys Euryn — Bryn Euryn — Llys Euryn
Cottage — Llandrillo-yn-Rhos Church

Summary
This short walk rises 100 metres to a summit. The route down includes a short
scramble which can be bypassed.

Attractions
The shortest walk in the book starts by the church at Llandrillo-yn-Rhos (church of
St Trillo, on the moor), but an interesting extension can be made before or after the
walk, down Church Road to the beach where a little chapel is built around St Trillo's
Well. Communion is held there at 8.00 am each morning.

The church tower is unusual in that it was used as part of a system of 16th century
watchtowers around the coast of Britain. This linked, to the west, with a tower at
Deganwy, and to the east, with the watchtower above Abergele.

Watchtowers were manned in case of pirate raids or attacks from other countries.
Beacons, using burning pitch, were lit to carry warnings along the coast (see route 1).

On the route you pass a fortified medieval hall, Llys Euryn, now a ruin but with
a tall standing chimney. The hall belonged to a famous Conwy family, ancestors of
the Tudor kings of England.

For a small hill, only 131 metres above sea level, there are magnificent views.
Look above Colwyn Bay to see Pwllycrochan Woods and turn clockwise for a
panorama of Snowdonia, Conwy Mountain, Anglesey and Puffin Island, Great Orme,
and Little Orme.

If you can't see any of these it is either because of the poor weather or perhaps
you need some of the tiny white flowers that grow on the hill. This is eyebright and
was once used as a herbal remedy for eye complaints.

Refreshments
There are lots of cafes along the promenade at the foot of Church Road, while The
Ship sells food and liquid refreshment during opening times.

Route 10

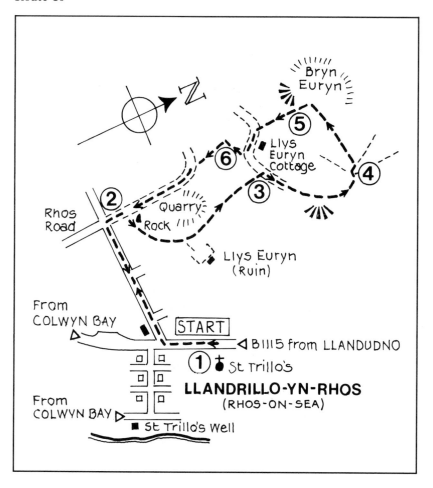

Route 10

Bryn Euryn   1 mile

Start

Llandrillo-yn-Rhos (Rhos-on-Sea) Church, GR SH832805. There are six coastal bus routes passing the church. The nearest train station is at Colwyn Bay, then either take the bus or walk along the prom (one mile each way) and turn right up Church Road, just past St Trillo's Well. Cars can park in the lay-by by The Ship on the B1115.

Route

1. *After looking up the church tower, leave the churchyard, turn left and follow the road along to The Ship, but turn right before it, along Tan-y-bryn Road.*

2. *Take the track on your right, opposite Rhos Road. Turn right by the rock and follow the path past the ruin of the stone hall.*

3. *When you reach the wide track turn right.*

4. *Beyond the large clearing (with the seat) continue through gorse and bear left to a five-way junction (with a stone marked 6). Take the ascending path to the summit.*

5. *Return towards the church and the sea. The path descends steeply (so you can return on your outward path, then continue along the wide track if you want to avoid the scramble).*

6. *Just beyond Llys Euryn Cottage (or before it if you avoided the steep path) turn downhill and keep to the main path. Turn left at the track and retrace your steps along Tan-y-bryn Road.*

A sea wall

The re-discovery of the Great Orme Mines

Great Orme

Outline
Llandudno Pier − Happy Valley − Mynydd Isaf − St Tudno's Church − headland − Summit Station − Great Orme Mines − Llandudno

Summary
Climb through the ornamental park on to the limestone hill above, before you take a level walk around the peninsula to the Summit Station and return by foot, or tram, to the town.

Attractions
Get away from the bustle of Llandudno's town and beach through the Happy Valley Park. There is a Gorsedd (stone circle commemorating the National Eisteddfod) in the park, and a camera obscura overlooking the town above the cable car station.

If granny will leave the ornamental park, and the children leave the play equipment, you need to get them both past the toboggan run, although if you leave enough time to wait in the queue, perhaps it would be a good opportunity to have a go yourself.

Up on Mynydd Isaf (lowest mountain) there are views of the bay and the coastline towards Liverpool. The path takes you past a small well, Ffynnon Powell, to St Tudno's Church where, if you arrive on a Sunday morning in summer, you may see an outdoor service or just the sheep acting as ecofriendly lawnmowers around the gravestones.

Further along, beside the dry Ffynnon Rufeinig (Roman well) are strips of ridge and furrow farming left from medieval times. A short diversion down Hwylfa'r Ceirw (the path of the deer) leads to the limestone foundations of a large rectangular medieval hall.

Natural outcrops of rock forming 'limestone pavements' support a variety of plants. Look for wild marjoram, harebell, parsley fern, the small purple flowers of wild thyme, and the yellow flowers of rockrose, as well as tiny 'bonsai' trees stunted by the lack of soil: all are hidden in the grykes (crevices).

Near the Summit Station, the terminus of the tram and cable car, is a Visitor Centre giving information about the Great Orme.

Purple heather and yellow gorse on white limestone; images of the Great Orme that must have made an impression on humankind for thousands of years. Over four thousand years ago people made an impression on the Orme, quarrying and tunnelling to reach the valuable copper crystal that may have been purified, and then traded from here all over Europe. On your return journey, which can be made on foot or by tram, stop by the Halfway Station. Here, you can go underground and back in time 5,000 years at the Great Orme Mines, perhaps one of the most interesting archaeological finds in Britain, and the largest mine of its type in the world.

Route 11

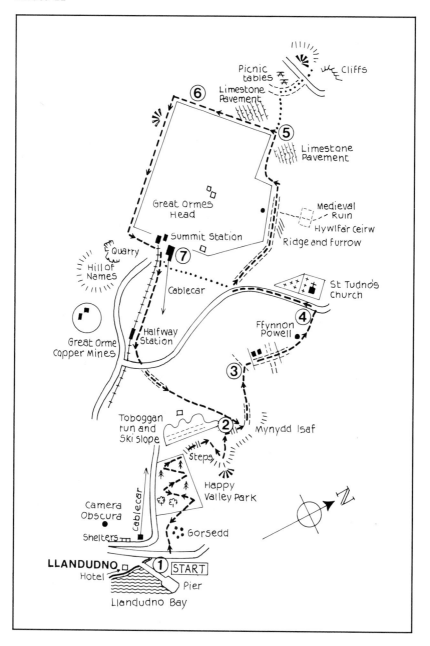

Route 11

Great Orme   3 or 5 miles

Start

*Llandudno Pier, GR SH736773. Trains to Llandudno. Buses along the coast.
Parking throughout the town or in signed car parks.*

Alternatives

*The shorter route goes direct to the Summit Station from St Tudno's Church
(direction 3). Another way to shorten either route by a mile is to return from the
summit by tram or cable car. An extension to the cliffs (direction 4) lengthens the
longer route by only half a mile.*

Route

1. *Follow the coast road 200 metres to Happy Valley. Fork up the steps on your left
   and head past the stones into the ornamental park. Leave by the gate at the top
   right-hand corner and continue up wide limestone steps.*

2. *After diverting to the minor summit on your right, continue along the main path.
   At the top of the steps keep on the main path to the right.*

3. *In 400 metres keep right towards buildings, then go through the metal kissing gate
   and along the track ahead, towards St Tudno's Church.*

4. *Turn left at the lane and, in nearly 400 metres, turn right along the track, unless
   you wish to take the shorter route direct to the Summit Station ahead (then follow
   direction 6).*

5. *In less than a mile, at the sharp left-hand bend, you can extend your walk by taking
   the track to the cliffs ahead and returning here to continue but TAKE EXTREME
   CARE WITH CHILDREN AND ANIMALS NEAR THE CLIFF EDGES.*

6. *Continue along the path beside the wall for a mile to the Summit Station.*

7. *To return to the town on foot follow the tramway to the Halfway Station (the Great
   Orme Mines are on your right), then fork left along the stony track to the head of
   the ski slope and retrace your steps through Happy Valley Park.*

Refreshments

Ffynnon Powell supplies fresh water on the way, while the extension to the cliffs
(direction 4) passes picnic tables, although the limestone rocks make more natural
ones. There are shops, a cafe and bar at the Summit Station. Before or after the walk
you can find meals and snacks of all descriptions in Llandudno.

53

Hill of Names, Great Orme

Garreg Fawr and Drum

Outline
Llanfairfechan — golf course — Garreg Fawr (— Drum — Garreg Fawr) —
Nant y Felin — Llanfairfechan

Summary
Leaving the village below, the route climbs steadily towards the minor summit of
Garreg Fawr. The short walk returns down the northern slope, while the main route
circuits the summit — with a possible extension to Drum on the ridge above — before
returning down the northern slope.

Attractions
The route rises quickly out of the village giving good views over the sheep-cropped
landscape to Anglesey and Puffin Island. When the tide is out Lavan Sands, a nature
reserve, can be seen stretching to the Menai Strait.

  This walk is a good introduction to the mountains of Snowdonia and from the
circular route a long extension can be taken up to the high peak of Drum. The route
is on a stony track and returns the same way, so you can go as far as you wish, as
long as your family has time and energy to get down. The ridge is crossed at about
600 metres above sea level and reaches Drum at 770 metres. From there it continues
up the ridge to Foel Fras (942), Garnedd Uchaf (926) and Foel Grach (976), but this
would be a long-distance hike, not a family walk.

Refreshments
There is a fresh spring on the return journey, but otherwise this is a route for
sandwiches and Thermos flasks. In the village there is a cafe, a chip shop, a Chinese
take-away and also at least one pub which ''welcomes children''.

Route 12

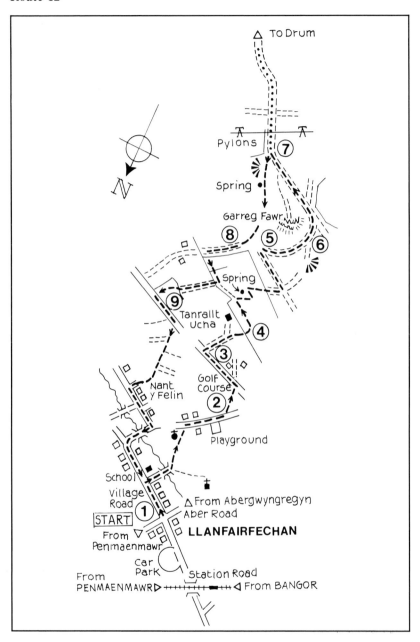

Route 12

Garreg Fawr and Drum   3, 5 or 10 miles

Start

Llanfairfechan traffic lights at the junction of Station Road, Aber Road and Village Road, GR SH682747. From the station turn right and right again up Station Road. Coastal buses stop near the lights. There is a car park on Station Road.

Alternatives

The shortest circular route goes to a viewpoint below the summit of Garreg Fawr, while the longer route skirts the summit before returning. The long linear extension leaves the circular route and ascends to Drum. There is no need to decide which route to take until you reach the clearly marked choices in the text.

Route

1. *Follow Village Road, then turn right before the school. Take the path across the river and turn left. At the road use the kissing gate and turn right. Continue along Llanerch Road.*

2. *Fifty metres beyond the playground turn left through an iron kissing gate. Stay beside the right-hand hedge of the golf course until you reach the lane. Turn left.*

3. *Just before the end of the golf course turn right up the tarmac track to Tanrallt Ucha. Before the gateway at the top, fork right. Use the ladder stile on to the mountain.*

4. *Turn left and follow the old ploughing ridges for only 100 metres, then, just beyond the farm, turn sharp right. Follow the green track steeply uphill past a spring (probably the former water supply to the farm). Stay on the wide rutted zigzag track and go through the iron kissing gate. In 100 metres turn left at the crossing tracks, ignoring the waymark for the North Wales Path.*

5. *When you reach the wall corner the shortest route goes ahead over the ladder stile (go on to direction 8). For the main route, and the extension, turn sharp right before the ladder stile to pass below the summit of Carreg Fawr.*

6. *Before the wall, tracks join from your right. Beyond the wall, keep on the higher track. (In a hundred metres or so a small trodden path leads to the summit. This is not a recorded right of way. If you leave the path and approach the rocks, return here to continue).*

7. *Before the pylons and the wall corner turn sharp left for your descent (unless you wish to take the track ahead on to the higher ridge and Drum, returning to this point on the same track). Descend a kilometre to cross the ladder stile seen earlier.*

8. *Go down the track and over another ladder stile on your left before the gate. After 350 metres and another ladder stile take one on your right and descend the walled track to the lane.*

9. *Turn left, then in 100 metres turn right down the narrow lane and ignore turns to left and right. Continue along the road. Turn left when you reach the T-junction. At the next T-junction cross the bridge and go downhill to the traffic lights.*

The Pier Head at Llandudno

Foel Lûs and Druids' Circle

Outline
Penmaenmawr – Mountain Lane – Foel Lus – Druids' Circle –
Graiglwyd Farm – Penmaenmawr

Summary
A steep ascent climbs 200 metres up a tarmac lane. The shorter walk then circuits the
hill and returns down the lane, while the longer route stays on the level and returns
on a hillside path. Both are easy walking on clear tracks.

Attractions
The hills rise dramatically behind the village of Penmaenmawr, and your initial climb
is rewarded by tremendous views of the coast, including Anglesey, Penmon
Lighthouse and Puffin Island to the north-west, Great Orme and Conwy Mountain to
the north-east. Go up at the end of August or the beginning of September to see the
heather in its full regal purple glory. A small man-made cave beside the track,
possibly the remains of a trial dig for limestone, adds interest or gives shelter from
bad weather. If you have not yet done the route from Dwygyfylchi try tracing this
from your 'aerial' viewpoint using the route map.

Beyond Foel Lus you can head back or continue past Welsh smallholdings to the
impressive Druids' Circle, but other smaller stone circles can be seen on the way.
These were probably burial mounds from Neolithic times.

One large boulder, I suggested to my son, is undoubtedly a giant's seat, and from
it you can see the Druids' Circle and also look south across the moorland at the
impressive bulk of Tal y Fan. Experienced walkers can leave the main route and
follow a track by the wall opposite, which forks left beside the wall and heads across
the moor to this ridge, returning by the same path (1 mile each way).

Refreshments
Available in Penmaenmawr village; none en-route.

Route 13

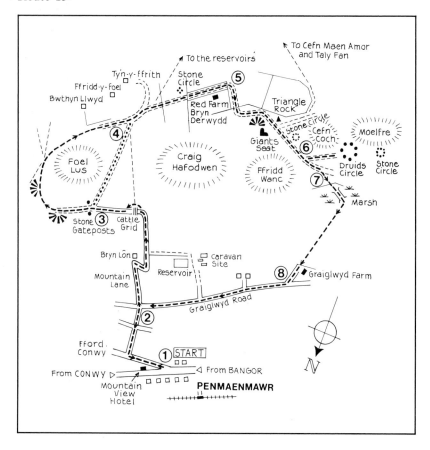

Route 13

Foel Lûs and Druid's Circle   3 or 5 miles

Start

Penmaenmawr, Mountain View Hotel, GR SH720763. Trains on the coast line. Coastal buses pass through the village. Parking on side roads nearby.

Alternatives

The three mile route follows directions 1-4 only. There is no need to decide which way to go until you reach direction 4. From the longer route an extension of three miles to Cefn Maen Amor, the ridge north-west of Tal y Fan with a clear path to the summit can be made by experienced walkers across the clear moorland path (see Attractions), but only the start of this is shown on the route map and no further directions are given in the text below.

Route

1. *From the Hotel follow Ffordd Conwy and turn first right up Groesffordd Lane. Cross a road and continue uphill.*

2. *Cross the next road and continue up Mountain Lane. (In about a kilometre a signed path leads to the right and soon descends to the village for those who want a very short walk. Follow direction 8 at the lane).*

3. *Beyond the cattle grid, at the corner of the lane go ahead between the stone columns and follow the track. Around the hill, at the five-way junction, turn right beside the telephone wires. Pass the smallholding by continuing ahead along the track by the stone wall.*

4. *At the track junction the shorter route turns right and returns down Mountain Lane. For the longer route turn left, then fork right along the track.*

5. *Beyond Red Farm (also named Bryn Derwydd − druids' hill) keep on the track and keep right at the junction by the 'giant's seat'.*

6. *At the next track junction fork right for the return walk. To visit Druids' Circle fork left, then retrace your steps.*

7. *Descend and fork right through the kissing gate. In 200 metres, just past the bridge, fork right downhill. In half a mile take the track leaving the farm on your left.*

8. *Turn right along the lane and continue along Graiglwyd Road to the foot of Mountain Lane. Descend to the main road.*

61

The Observatory, Prestatyn

Vale of Clwyd — a view from route 14

Gwaenysgor and Bishop's Wood

Outline
Prestatyn — Observatory — Offa's Dyke Path — Gwaenysgor — Bishop's-wood —
Walkway — (Roman Bath house) — Prestatyn

Summary
A steep climb on Offa's Dyke Path takes you above a limestone escarpment from
where you can walk into the quiet village of Gwaenysgor. The return route through
woodland is also fairly steep, so take care in wet weather when the path can become
slippery, and ensure that you are wearing suitable footwear.

Attractions
The observatory in a private house on the Prestatyn hillside was used until the First
World War, when it was dismantled on the orders of the army. Lights had been seen
in the dome and it was suggested that these could be signals to U-boats thought to be
in Llandudno Bay awaiting escaped prisoners-of-war.

Offa's Dyke Path here is nowhere near the dyke (which ends near Mold) and the
path does not join the dyke until it reaches Chirk. When the path was given its name
it was believed that another dyke on the hills above was part of the 8th century Offa's
Dyke, but this has now proved to be of 12th century origin and has been renamed the
Whitford Dyke. The path, however, runs 168 miles to Chepstow in South Wales. This
family walk uses less than a mile of it.

The limestone escarpment, apart from having spectacular views of the Vale of
Clwyd, is also noted for its range of limestone-loving plants. Some, like the orchids,
live a precarious existence, so please do not pick any; a sunny day is ideal for
sketching or photos. There is a profusion of hart's-tongue fern on the lower part of
the walk, while the upper rocks are covered with the yellow flowers of rock-rose in
early summer.

The village of Gwaenysgor is famous for its parish registers, which are the oldest
intact records of this type and date from the days of Henry VIII.

The legend of a lord from medieval times who managed to have his illegitimate
child adopted by his wife, with the tale that the baby had been found in an eagle's
nest, is said to be the reason for the name of the village pub, the Eagle and Child.

As you descend the woodland path through Coed yr Esgob (Bishop's-wood) you
pass the entrance to the 'Fishmine', so called, it is said, because the former spoil heap
at its entrance resembled a plaice. If you want to explore this, a torch and wellingtons
would be needed. Note, however, that in 1993 when several adventurous boys took
an inflatable dinghy inside to reach the island across the lake, they were stranded when
the boat became punctured and had to be rescued by officers of the fire service who
had to wade through the freezing water to save them.

Continued on page 66

63

Route 14

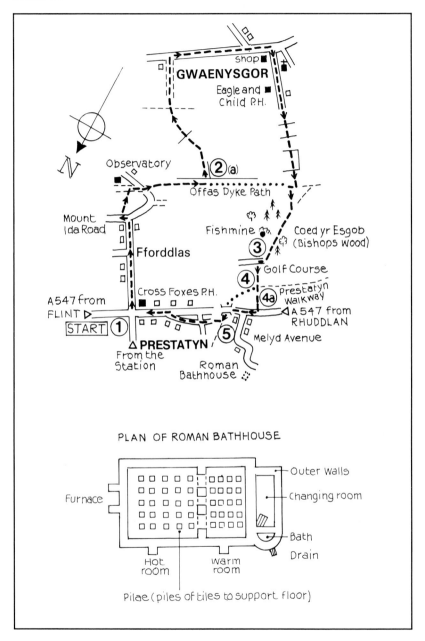

PLAN OF ROMAN BATHHOUSE

Furnace

Outer walls

Changing room

Bath

Drain

Hot room

Warm room

Pilae (piles of tiles to support floor)

Route 14

Gwaenysgor and Bishop's Wood   2 or 3 miles

Start
The Cross Foxes PH, High Street, Prestatyn, GR SJ068825. Coastal buses and trains go to Prestatyn. Parking in the town car parks. The Cross Foxes is at the top of the High Street at the A547 junction.

Alternatives
For the shorter route omit direction 2 and follow 2a. To see the bath house omit direction 4 and follow 4a.

Route
1. *Follow the Offa's Dyke 'acorn' sign up Fforddlas beside the Cross Foxes. At the first sharp bend ascend the path a few yards into Mount Ida Road. When you reach the crossing lane by the observatory turn right, right again at the road, then first left up the Offa's Dyke Path. Ignore paths to the left.*

2. *For the main routes at the crest of the hill, when the path begins to descend, take the stile on your left. Follow the path around the hill, through woodland and along the track and lane to the road. Turn right, and turn right again at the village shop. At the end of the road, cross the stile and follow the signposted path across the fields ahead. Descend 50 metres to the Offa's Dyke Path, turn right and take the first path on your left, down through the woods. (Ignore direction 2a).*

2a. *For the short route continue along the escarpment on the Offa's Dyke Path until the next signposted path on your right; descend this through the woods.*

3. *Beyond the Fishmine, at the foot of the path, go on to the lane, but in only a few yards go down steps and follow the path across the golf course.*

4. *To return directly to Prestatyn turn right along the crossing track: the Prestatyn Walkway. (Ignore direction 4a).*

4a. *To visit the Roman bath house continue across the golf course to the road. BEWARE, THE STEPS GO DIRECTLY ON TO THE BUSY ROAD. Turn right, then left down Melyd Avenue. The bath house is at the foot of the road. To return to the town centre retrace your steps up Melyd Avenue, turn left at the main road, then drop down on to the Prestatyn Walkway just before the bridge. Turn left.*

5. *At the wide crossing path turn right and follow the main road ahead to the Cross Foxes.*

An optional short road walk is necessary to visit the Roman bath house, excavated in 1984 by the Clwyd-Powys Archaeological Trust. Under the site around the remains were found 13 timber buildings. In the bath house the pilae (stacks of bricks) under the hypocaust (underfloor heating system) still show the casting marks of the Roman brickworks and were probably made at the Roman tile and brick works at BOVIVM (Holt) ten Roman miles upriver from DEVA (Chester). The baths consisted of a hot room, a warm room and a changing room with cold plunge attached. The site is assumed to be a civil settlement with military connections and was probably used as a base for mining the lead from the limestone hills.

The last part of the walk is along the Prestatyn-Dyserth Walkway, actually a disused railway, closed to passengers in 1930 and completely in 1973. It was part of the London and North Western Railways network.

Refreshments

At the start and end of the walk the Cross Foxes has a children's menu and serves vegetarian food. Check on 01745 854984 before visiting as the pub changes meals out of season. The Eagle and Child at Gwaenysgor, however, will only let children in the garden. There are several cafes and pubs in Prestatyn.

Rhuddlan Castle

66

Rhuddlan Castle and Twt Hill

Outline
Rhyl − River Clwyd − Rhuddlan Castle − Twt Hill − River Clwyd − Rhyl

Summary
If you expect a rugged terrain do not go on this route. This is almost the only walk that can be taken from the tourist resort of Rhyl and is therefore well used with clear tracks. The banks of the river are in an exposed position and the walk can be windy.

Attractions
The main feature of this walk is the castle, but those who are interested in birdlife will find the mudflats of the river rewarding, especially in late summer and winter. Binoculars and a spotter's or field guide would be advantageous.

Gulls, crows, waders and wildfowl feed here when the tide is out. Blackheaded and herring gull are common. Oystercatcher, ringed and grey plover, and curlew can be seen near the estuary, while further up the river look for cormorant and shelduck, tufted duck and occasional black-throated diver, redshank and greenshank. Where the river is calmer you may spot pied or grey wagtail and, if you are lucky, the blue flash of a kingfisher.

Rhuddlan is the site of Edward I's second Welsh castle (the first is at Flint), but is also the site of a Norman wooden castle; a motte and bailey. William the Conqueror's Domesday Book of 1086 records that Robert of Roelent (Rhuddlan) held 'half of the castle, the church, the iron mines, the river, the fisheries, mills, tolls and unclaimed forests of the area', whilst Earl Hugh of Chester held the other half. Twt Hill is the site of the wooden castle.

Before the Normans came, Earl Harold of Wessex held the town. He had captured it from Gryffydd ap Llewellyn, a Welsh prince who had his palace here. Saxon ditch and dyke defences have been found in the south-east part of the town, leading to the suggestion that Rhuddlan was formerly Cledmutha (Clwydmouth) mentioned in the Anglo-Saxon Chronicles of 921 AD.

Interesting buildings on the walk include Abbey Farm, which was the site of Rhuddlan Friary built in the 13th century by Dominican or Black Friars, and Parliament Building, said by some to be where Edward I issued his Statute of Wales, which created the counties of Wales that lasted until re-organisation in 1974.

Refreshments
Cafes and take-aways litter the streets of Rhyl and there are also a few in Rhuddlan, so you will never be far from food or drink. If you picnic by the river remember to take a portion for the ducks.

Route 15

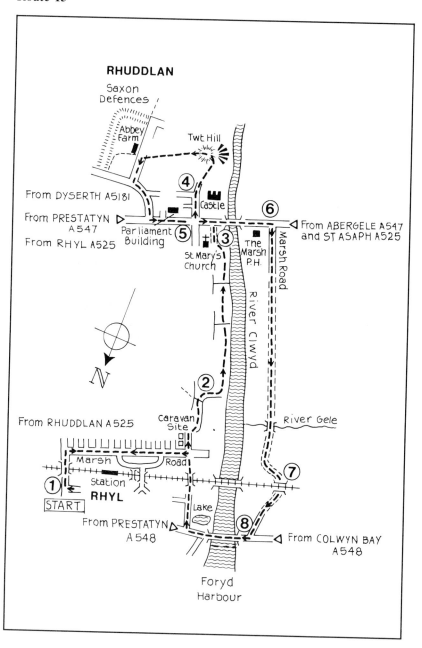

Route 15

Rhuddlan Castle and Twt Hill   2½ or 5 miles

Start
Rhyl Railway Station, GR SJ009812. Coastal trains and buses. Town car parks.

Alternative
Get the bus back from Rhuddlan (see direction 5) for the short route.

Route
1. *From the station cross the road bridge and turn right along Marsh Road. By the railway footbridge near the far end of the road, turn left into the cul-de-sac. Fork right at the end and follow the footpath around the fence for over half a mile to reach the River Clwyd.*

2. *Follow the river embankment for 1 mile.*

3. *Drop down to the track below the church. At the main road turn left, then right along Castle Road.*

4. *Follow Hylas Lane and the footpath to visit Twt Hill. Continue along the path and turn left at the road (opposite Abbey Farm). Turn left on to Princes Road at the T-junction. Turn left at the main road to pass Parliament Building.*

5. *To return to Rhyl by bus, cross the road to the bus stop. To continue by foot follow the main road over the bridge.*

6. *Beyond The Marsh public house turn right and follow Marsh Road, later a track, to the Railway Viaduct at Rhyl.*

7. *Go under the railway bridge and continue to the coast road.*

8. *Turn right, cross the bridge and follow the road beside the lake. Turn right and go to the end of Westbourne Avenue. Cross the railway footbridge back into Marsh Road, and retrace your steps to the start.*

Ewloe Castle

Ewloe Castle and Wepre Country Park

Outline
Shotton Station – Killins Lane – Ewloe Castle – Wepre Park – Shotton Station

Summary
Just behind the busy main road going through Deeside is an area of hill and woodland. Thus, at the end of a quiet estate road, you gradually climb through farmland. After a short stepped climb to the castle the return route is downhill through woodland and alongside the Wepre Brook.

Attractions
A small nature reserve near the start of the walk is managed by the Deeside Urban Wildlife Group. The area, which also contains a children's park, was once a rubbish tip, the only reminders being the several green poles surmounted by wind vanes, erected to prevent the build-up of methane gas.

Above Killins Lane there are views over Deeside and Chester. Look for the spire of Chester's town hall next to the tower of the city's cathedral. Beyond are the sandstone ridges of the Cheshire Hills.

The Welsh castle of Llewelyn ap Gruffydd stands in a commanding position above the Wepre Brook, but in the 13th century there may not have been any trees here to hide the view. Edward I took the castle in his first campaign during 1276. In 1277 he cleared trees from his coastal roads and defences by employing a thousand woodmen for the job.

The fact that Wepre was already a small area of importance had been noted in two entries in William the Conqueror's Domesday Book. This tells us that a free Saxon 'Earnwig' had held (part) of the land before 1066 and that after the invasion the Norman 'William' held it, and that (part of) the land belonged to the church. There was arable land of about 50 hectares (about 130 acres) which was taxed. Within the population of twenty or so, the men were listed as a rider, three villagers and two boarders. One entry records that 'There is a wood one league long and half a league wide'.

The Visitor Centre is built near the site of the late eighteenth century Wepre Hall, and remains of the ornamental trees and gardens can be found in the woodland. A stone bridge of the same period lies on the brook below. Information about the hall, and its occupants through two centuries, can be found in the Visitor Centre, which is open in the daytime at week-ends and irregularly in the week (see the appendices). Golf clubs can be hired at the golf course, and there is a children's play area nearby.

Refreshments
There are shops and cafes in Shotton and a snack bar beside the golf course in Wepre Park. Picnic tables can be found near the main path through the park and a 'litter man' in the Visitor Centre is a reminder to take your rubbish home with you.

Route 16

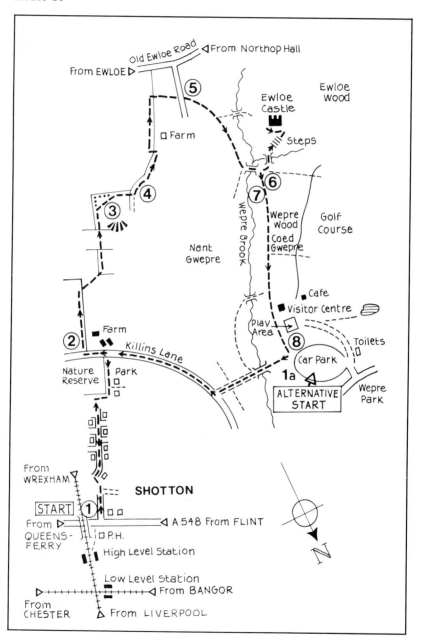

Route 16

Ewloe Castle and Wepre Country Park   3 miles

Start

Shotton Station, GR SJ307688. Trains on the Wrexham-Biston and the Chester-Holyhead lines. Buses: Coastliner and Deeside services.

ALTERNATIVE START − Parking is available at Wepre Country Park and some buses pass the entrance, GR SJ295384. Follow directions starting at 1a, and omit direction 8.

Route

1. *From the station entrance follow the roadway opposite, and the path at the end. Continue ahead along the estate road and follow this, ignoring turns left and right. At the end of the road follow the path and bear right at the T-junction. Pass the children's playground and the nature reserve to reach Killins Lane by a farm. Turn left. (Ignore direction 1a).*

1a. *From the end of the car park take the path downhill, cross the bridge and follow the main path ahead. When you reach Killins Lane turn right to reach a farm.*

2. *Turn right up the signed path beside the farm and cross the next stile on the right at the end of the field. Bear half-left across the field and, beyond another stile turn left. Go straight ahead through the next field and into the one following.*

3. *At the top of the rise, when the field levels out, turn half-right to a stile. (If cropped the farmer leaves a path around the field).*

4. *Turn left along the green lane and then stay beside the field boundary to use the kissing gate at the next corner, but continue in the same direction. Ignore a gate on your right, but take the next stile on the right and go ahead to a kissing gate at the lane.*

5. *Take the kissing gate opposite into Wepre Park. Keep on the main path to cross the stone bridge.*

6. *From here cross the wooden bridge and ascend to the Ewloe Castle returning to this point to continue the route.*

7. *Follow the path downstream to the Visitor Centre and, unless you wish to explore other paths or the lake in the park, make your way to the car park beyond the play area.*

8. *From the end of the car park take the path downhill, cross the bridge and follow the main path ahead. When you reach Killins Lane turn right to reach the farm. Turn left along the path and retrace your steps to the station.*

Extinct action at Dinosaur World, Colwyn Bay

Still life at the Farm Museum, Greenfield Valley (Route 9)

Useful information

Appendices

Routes in order of difficulty

None of these walks is difficult for a reasonably fit person, so this list is mainly in order of distance.

Route 10	—	1½ miles	Route 1 — 3 miles
Route 8	—	2 miles	Route 2 — 3 miles
Route 15	—	2½ miles	Route 3 — 4 miles
Route 4	—	2 miles	Route 1 — 4 miles
Route 6	—	2 miles	Route 4 — 2½ miles
Route 14	—	2 miles	Route 5 — 4 miles
Route 7	—	2½ miles	Route 12 — 5 miles
Route 11	—	3 miles	Route 15 — 5 miles
Route 13	—	3 miles	Route 13 — 5 miles
Route 12	—	3 miles	Route 11 — 5 miles
Route 9	—	3 miles	Route 8 — 5 miles
Route 14	—	3 miles	Route 3 — 5 miles
Route 16	—	3 miles	Route 4 — 4 miles
Route 8	—	3 miles	Route 5 — 7 miles
Route 5	—	2 miles	Route 12 — 10 miles

Public Transport

Remember to check return times before you start.

Trains
British Rail Llandudno Junction 01492 585151
Liverpool 0151 709 9696
Holyhead 01407 769222
Buses
Crosville Wales Rhyl 01745 343721
Bangor 01248 370295
Llandudno 01492 596969
Mold 01352 700250
Aberystwyth 01970 617951

Bus and train timetables are available from Tourist Information Offices.

Anglice

The following pronunciations of Welsh words are given in Anglice to avoid potential embarrassment for non-Welsh speakers on buses, etc; emphasis is on the syllable in capitals:

Abergele	Aber-GEL-ay
Dwygyfylchi	Dwee-guv-UL-key
Ffynnongroyw	Fun-on-grow
Gwaenysgor	Gwun-US-gor
Llandrillo	Hlan-DRIhlo
Llandudno	Hlan-DID-no
Llanfairfechan	Hlan-via-VEK-an
Penmaenmawr	Pen-MINE-mawer
Rhuddlan	RITH-lan

Tourist Information Offices

Ewloe – 01244 541597
Colwyn Bay – 01492 530478
Conwy – 01492 592248
Llandudno – 01492 876413
Rhos-on-Sea – 01492 548778
Rhyl promenade – 01745 355068
Prestatyn – 01745 889092

Where to go and what to see

Abergele and Pensarn – A quiet town and a seaside village between Rhyl and Colwyn Bay, the village has a sandy beach below the pebbles by the sea wall and only a few amusement arcades, with a children's go-kart track. The 19th century ruin of Gwrych Castle stands above the town, giving it a fairy-tale image.
Leisure Centre: Faenol Avenue, 01745 733677.

Bagillt
Focus Cinema: High Street, 01352 715670.

Bangor – This university city of North Wales is at the entrance to Anglesey/Ynys Mon and connected by Telford's famous Menai Bridge.
Museum and Art Gallery: Fford Gwynedd. Tue-Fri 12.30-4.30, Sat 10.30-4.30. 01248 353368.
Theatr Gwynedd: Deiniol Road. 01248 351707.
Arfon Sports Hall: 01248 351697.
Bangor Pier Maritime Centre: Admission charge. 01248 372284.
Penrhyn Castle: Neo-medieval castle, railway museum with full size engines, old masters' gallery, special events. End March-end Oct (exc Tue) 12.00-5.00 house, 11.00-7.00 grounds. Jul-Aug 1 hour earlier. Admission charge, free to NT members. 01248 353084.
Plaza Cinema: High Street, 01248 362059.

Bodelwyddan – Much of this village beside the A55 was formerly a private estate. Buses run from Rhyl May-Sept.
Marble Church: Magnificent limestone church with marble interior.
Bodelwyddan Castle: Portraits, Puzzle Gallery, Victorian Extravaganza, adventure woodland, gardens. Apr-end Oct 10.00-5.00 (exc Fri Apr-end Jun, Sep-end Oct), 01745 584060.

Colwyn Bay – This Victorian resort town has a long sandy beach and good shopping centre.
Princess Cinema: Princes Drive. 01492 532557.
Welsh Mountain Zoo (signposted and bus from town): Tarzan Trail, endangered species, children's farm, special events. Mid Mar-end Oct 9.30-5.00, winter (exc Christmas Day) 9.30-4.00.
Eirias Park: Leisure pool, squash, tennis; seasonal: boating, mini-golf, bowling. 01492 533223.
Dinosaur World: Eirias Park. Easter-end Oct 10.00-6.00. Admission charge. 01492 518111.
Harlequin Puppet Theatre: Cayley Promenade, Rhos-on-Sea. 01492 548166.
Theatr Colwyn: 01492 532668.
Hwylfan Dafydd Farm & Riding Centre: Llysfaen. Farm animals, pony trekking. Easter-end Oct 9.00-6.00, Nov-Mar (exc Christmas Day, Boxing Day) 10.00-4.00. 01492 516965.

Conwy Valley – The medieval walled town of Conwy is dominated by the castle, with the quay a close runner-up.

Conwy Castle: Castle interior, exhibitions, shop. Mid March-end Oct 9.30-6.30, winter 9.30-4.00, Suns 9.00-2.00. Admission charge. 01492 592358.

Visitor Centre: Near castle. Brass rubbing, exhibition, video. Small admission charge to exhibition. 01492 592358.

Butterfly Jungle: Bodlondeb Park by walls. Exotic plants, tropical birds, live tropical butterflies. Apr-Sept 10.00-5.30, Oct 10.00-4.00. Admission charge. 01492 650460.

Aberconwy House: Castle Street. Period museum. Easter-end Oct (exc Tue) 11.00-5.30. Admission charge. Free to NT members. 01492 592246.

Bodnant Garden: Tal-y-Cafn, Conwy Valley on A470. 80 acres of garden, cafe, nursery. Mid March-end Oct 10.00-5.00. Admission charge. 01492 650460.

Pinewood Riding Stables: 01492 592256. **Smallest House:** On the quay. Admission charge.

Deeside

Wepre Park: Visitor Centre, golf course, nature trail, special events. Open all year, Visitor Centre at week-ends.

Deeside Leisure Centre: Queensferry. Includes ice rink. 01244 812311.

Deeside Ski Slope: Kelsterton Road, Connah's Quay. 01244 822215.

Flint

Castle: Open to the public all year.

Holywell & Greenfield Valley – A small town which grew on the fame of St Winefride's Well is near the heritage valley with its industrial and religious ruins.

Abbey Farm & Visitor Centre: Greenfield Valley Heritage Park (signposted). Agricultural Museum, animals, special events. End March-end Oct 10.00-5.00, 01352 714172.

Basingwerk Abbey: Greenfield Valley (signposted). Ruin open all year.

St Winefride's Well: (Signposted). Open all year. 01352 713054.

Leisure Centre: Fron Park. 01352 712027.

Llandudno – Floods damaged many of the lower rooms of shops and hotels in the town during the winter of 1992, but this tourist resort was back in business by the spring. There are a variety of restaurants and amusements, while donkeys still give rides on the beach.

Great Orme Mines: Near tramway Halfway Station. Prehistoric copper mines, video, shop, cafe. Apr-Oct 9.00-5.00. 01492 870447.

Great Orme Tramway: Victoria Station. Trams to Summit Station Apr-Oct 10.00-6.00.

Oriel Mostyn Gallery: 01492 879201.

Ski Llandudno: Wyddfyd Road. 01492 874707.

Summit Complex: 01492 860963.

Mercier Fine Art Gallery: 3a Oxford Road. 01492 870081.

Arcadia Theatre: Aberconwy Centre, The Promenade. 01492 879771.

Palladium Cinema: Gloddaeth Street. 01492 876244.

Motor Cycle Museum: Bodhyfryd Road. 01492 870424.

Prestatyn – Only one main street means that the town is quieter than nearby Rhyl. At one end of the street is the beach, and at the other end Offa's Dyke Path leads into the hills.

North Wales Bowls: Ffrith Beach. Indoor flat green bowling. 01745 886100.

Nova: Central Beach. Swim, dance, wine and dine. 01745 888021.

Scala Cinema: 01745 845365.

Rhuddlan – Based on a Saxon burgh and laid out beside the castle built by Edward I, Rhuddlan is set between the tourist resort of Rhyl and green meadows in the Vale of Clwyd.

Castle: Admission charge. 01745 590777.

Twt Hill: Near the castle (signposted). Site of Robert of Rhuddlan's motte and bailey. Open to the public all year.

Rhyl − Shops, amusement arcades, a boating lake and a fair − in season Rhyl is one of the busiest towns on the coast.

Knights Cavern: 38-41 West Parade. Torture chambers, Welsh legends, audio-visual. Apr-Sept daily 10.00-10.00, Oct-end March 11.00-6.00. Admission charge. 01745 338562.

Sun Centre: The Promenade. Swimming, surfing, tropical rainstorms, children's pool, 60 metre slide. 01745 344433.

Sky Tower: Easter-Sept 10.00-5.00. 01745 331071.

Superbowl: 102 West Parade. 01745 342247.

New Pavilion Theatre: East Prom. 01745 330000.

Coliseum Theatre: West Prom. 01745 351126.

Rhyl Town Hall (Theatre): Wellington Road. 01745 337480.

Little Theatre: Vale Road. 01745 342229.

Sea Life Centre: East Parade. British marine life, restaurant, shop. All year 10.00-5.00 (exc Christmas Day), summer holidays 9.00-6.00. 01745 344660.

Apollo Cinema: Brighton Road. 01745 353856.

Quasar: 102 West Parade. Laser tag. 01745 342247.

Maps and Guides

1:50,000 OS Landranger Series
115 Snowdon & surrounding area
116 Denbigh & Colwyn Bay area
117 Chester, Wrexham & surrounding area

1:25,000 OS Pathfinder Series
751 SH 47/57 Bangor & Llangefni
752 SH 67 Llanfairfechan
736 SH 78/88 Llandudno
753 SH 77/87 Conwy & Colwyn Bay
754 SH 97 Abergele
737 SJ 08/18 Rhyl
755 SJ 07/17 Holywell
756 SJ 27/37 Ellesmere Port (West)
773 SJ 26/36 Mold (Yr Wyddgrug) and Chester (West)

Walking guides available from Information Offices:
Llanfairfechan Walks. Aberconwy Borough Council.
Penmaenmawr Walks. Aberconwy Borough Council.
Circular walk No 1 Prestatyn-Gwaensygor-Graig Fawr. Clwyd County Council.
Circular walk No 2 Gwaenysgor-Trelawnyd-Golden Grove. Clwyd County Council.
Colwyn Bay Walks. Colwyn Bay Town Council.
Walks in Clwyd. 36 individual walks. Gordon Emery.
Family Walks in Snowdonia by Laurence Main. Scarthin Books.
Family Walks in Anglesey by Laurence Main. Scarthin Books.

Complaints about public footpaths

Footpaths, bridges, signposts, crops, etc, on public paths on the coast are dealt with by the Councils listed below. Please send a copy of any complaints to The Ramblers' Association.

Clwyd County Council, Director of Highways and Transportation, Shire Hall, Mold, Clwyd, CH7 6NF.

Copy to: Cyril Jones, RA Footpath Secretary (Clwyd), School House, Tremeirchion, St Asaph, Clwyd, LL17 0UN.

Gwynedd County Council, Council Offices, Caernarfon, Gwynedd, LL55 1SH.

Copy to: Frank Skelcey, RA Footpath Secretary (Gwynedd), 12 Gwydyr Road, Dolgarrog, Conwy, Gwynedd, LL32 8JS.

As from April 1996 there will be new unitary authorities for the North Wales coast but at the time of writing no addresses are available and the councils say that mail will be forwarded to the correct authority.

Walking groups in the area

Ramblers' Association, Bethesda Group: Jane Beddow, 5 Pen-y-bryn, Bethesda, Gwynedd, LL57 3BD. 01248 602194.

Ramblers' Association, Conwy Valley Group: Harry Ebbs, 9 Bryn Gannock, Deganwy, Conwy, Gwynedd. 01492 582402.

Ramblers' Association, Deeside Group: Liz Maxwell, 44 Willow Drive, Flint, Clwyd, CH6 5YJ. 01352 735539.

Ramblers' Association, Vale of Clwyd Group: Angie Devenport, Woodlands, Bishop's-wood Road, Prestatyn, Clwyd, LL19 9PL. 01745 888814.

Holywell Ramblers: Gwilym Morgan Meifod, Brynfod, Holywell, Clwyd, CH8 8AM. 01352 712181.

Abergele Ramblers: A Cropper, 12 Bryn Rhosin, Abergele. 01745 826997.

Gwynedd Ramblers: J Bradshaw, 1 Garth Wen, Llanfaes, Beaumaris, Gwynedd, LL58 8PJ. 01248 490397.

Prestatyn & District CHA Rambling Club: J Court, 16a East Avenue, Bryn Newydd, Prestatyn, LL19 9ES.

THE FAMILY WALKS SERIES

Family Walks on Anglesey. Laurence Main	ISBN 0 907758 66 5
Family Walks around Bakewell & Castleton. Norman Taylor	ISBN 0 907758 37 1
Family Walks in Berkshire & North Hampshire. Kathy Sharp	ISBN 0 907758 37 1
Family Walks around Bristol, Bath & the Mendips. Nigel Vile	ISBN 0 907758 19 3
Family Walks around Cardiff & the Valleys. Gordon Hindess	ISBN 0 907758 54 1
Family Walks in Cheshire. Chris Buckland	ISBN 0 907758 29 0
Family Walks in Cornwall. John Caswell	ISBN 0 907758 55 X
Family Walks in the Cotswolds. Gordon Ottewell	ISBN 0 907758 15 0
Family Walks in the Dark Peak. Norman Taylor	ISBN 0 907758 16 9
Family Walks in Dorset. Nigel Vile	ISBN 0 907758 86 X
Family Walks in East Sussex. Sally & Clive Cutter	ISBN 0 907758 71 1
Family Walks on Exmoor & the Quantocks. John Caswell	ISBN 0 907758 46 0
Family Walks in Gower. Amanda Green	ISBN 0 907758 63 0
Family Walks in Gwent. Gordon Hindess	ISBN 0 907758 87 8
Family Walks in Hereford and Worcester. Gordon Ottewell	ISBN 0 907758 20 7
Family Walks on the Isle of Man. John Kitto	ISBN 0 907758 91 6
Family Walks on the Isle of Wight. Laurence Main	ISBN 0 907758 56 8
Family Walks around Keswick and Northern Lakeland. Timothy and Sylvia Bunker	ISBN 0 907758 93 2
Family Walks in the Lake District. Barry McKay	ISBN 0 907758 40 1
Family Walks in Leicestershire. Meg Williams	ISBN 0 907758 82 7
Family Walks in Mendip, Avalon & Sedgemoor. Nigel Vile	ISBN 0 907758 41 X
Family Walks in Mid Wales. Laurence Main	ISBN 0 907758 27 4
Family Walks in the New Forest. Nigel Vile	ISBN 0 907758 60 6
Family Walks on the Norfolk Broads. Norman Taylor	ISBN 0 907758 90 8
Family Walks in Northamptonshire. Gordon Ottewell	ISBN 0 907758 81 9
Family Walks in the North Wales Borderlands. Gordon Emery	ISBN 0 907758 50 9
Family Walks on the North Wales Coast. Gordon Emery	ISBN 0 907758 89 4
Family Walks in North West Kent. Clive Cutter	ISBN 0 907758 36 3
Family Walks in North Yorkshire Dales. Howard Beck	ISBN 0 907758 52 5
Family Walks in Oxfordshire. Laurence Main	ISBN 0 907758 38 X
Family Walks in Pembrokeshire. Laurence Main	ISBN 0 907758 75 4
Family Walks in Snowdonia. Laurence Main	ISBN 0 907758 32 0
Family Walks in South Derbyshire. Gordon Ottewell	ISBN 0 907758 61 4
Family Walks in South Gloucestershire. Gordon Ottewell	ISBN 0 907758 33 9
Family Walks in South Shropshire. Marian Newton	ISBN 0 907758 30 4
Family Walks in South Yorkshire. Norman Taylor	ISBN 0 907758 25 8
Family Walks in the Staffordshire Peaks & Potteries. Les Lumsdon	ISBN 0 907758 34 7
Family Walks around Stratford & Banbury. Gordon Ottewell	ISBN 0 907758 49 5
Family Walks in Suffolk. C.J. Francis	ISBN 0 907758 64 9
Family Walks in Surrey. Norman Bonney	ISBN 0 907758 74 6
Family Walks around Swansea. Raymond Humphreys	ISBN 0 907758 62 2
Family Walks in the Teme Valley. Camilla Harrison	ISBN 0 907758 45 2
Family Walks in Three Peaks & Malham. Howard Beck	ISBN 0 907758 42 8
Family Walks in Warwickshire. Geoff Allen	ISBN 0 907758 53 3
Family Walks in the Weald of Kent & Sussex. Clive Cutter	ISBN 0 907758 51 7
Family Walks in West London. Caroline Bacon	ISBN 0 907758 72 X
Family Walks in West Sussex. Nich Channer	ISBN 0 907758 73 8
Family Walks in West Yorkshire. Howard Beck	ISBN 0 907758 43 6
Family Walks in the White Peak. Norman Taylor	ISBN 0 907758 09 6
More Family Walks in the White Peak. Norman Taylor	ISBN 0 907758 80 0
Family Walks in Wiltshire. Nigel Vile	ISBN 0 907758 21 5
Family Walks in the Wye Valley. Heather & Jon Hurley	ISBN 0 907758 26 6
Family Walks in Birmingham & West Midlands.	ISBN 0 907758 83 5

The publishers welcome suggestions for future titles and will be pleased to consider manuscripts relating to Derbyshire from new and established authors.

Scarthin Books of Cromford, in the Peak District, are also leading new, second-hand and antiquarian booksellers, and are eager to purchase specialised material, both ancient and modern.

Contact Dr. D.J. Mitchell 01629 823272.